Voices In My Heart

A collection of sacred poetry

StarShield Lortie

PURE PRESS

Pure Heart Press
Main Street Rag Publishing Company
Charlotte, North Carolina

Cover art designed by StarShield Lortie

ISBN 13: 978-1-59948-093-0
ISBN 10: 1-59948-093-X

Produced in the United States of America

Pure Heart Press
Main Street Rag Publishing Company
PO BOX 690100
Charlotte, NC 28227-7001
www.MainStreetRag.com

This book is dedicated to the Creative Spirit that lives at the core of all of us, to anyone who has the courage to reach for the dreams that dance wildly in the Heart. Love them enough to live them fully.

Ruth —
I am grateful for the 'mutual affection society'! What a gift you have been in my life. Thank you.

...and then the day came when
the risk to remain tight in a bud
was more painful than
the risk it took to blossom.

—Anais Nin

Contents

Notes to The Reader

While pursuing my personal writing practice and creating this book I termed the description "Sacred Writing" as a way to explain my personal style of writing. As I began using that term in the world the question would often come up "What is Sacred Writing?" While it feels a completely accurate description to me, it would take others in different directions. I use the term "Sacred Writing" to describe the use of writing as a way to connect to the sacredness in myself, to touch my own Spirit, to hear the voice of my heart.

Writing is something that we do everyday. Although most of us could never imagine what life would be like if we couldn't write, there is the tendency to take it for granted, allowing it no greater purpose than to communicate with another person.

Taken deeper, writing can tap into the truth and illuminate the mystery that lies in each of us. It can reveal You, touching the deepest recesses of your being, and bring forward all the possibilities of who you can become. The truth at the heart of each one of us speaks in many ways and writing is one way to connect with that voice and let it flow. Writing can explore your sense of the sacred, especially the sacredness of those dark places we often choose not to look at. It allows you to explore your quest for significance and purpose while providing a literal road for the application of your own personal experiences.

Utilized in this way, the act of writing is a sacred tool. Sacred Writing creates a road for the voice of the heart to travel, clarifying the way to create your life with your Spirit leading. It opens you to the subtle nuances of the movements of your own energy and allows for the development of your relationship with yourself and your relationship with the world.

Sacred writing is an endeavor that activates the creative spirit of the author, weaving a tapestry of story, song and vision that has dimension and color and emotion. The creation that evolves from the relationship of author and story touches the reader in different ways.

Sacred writing can be woven into one's daily spiritual practice as a way to deeply experience the divine uniqueness that is each of us. The poetry in this collection was born from me and has evolved in this manner.

Introduction

I began compiling this collection simply as a way for me to organize what I had written, so I could see it for myself and have some reference of what I had created. The more I collected and brought together these ideas and movements and revelations, the more they asked to be shared. Before I could second guess what I was doing, it evolved into the creation you now hold.

Initially this volume was intended as one very personal gift for one very rare person. Yet, the journey of putting everything together in actual book form opened something in me that I hadn't anticipated. Gifting the original book brought me to a sense of myself I hadn't touched in a very long time. I started writing more, and the more I wrote the more I wanted to write. Within a few months I had given out a few other copies as gifts. Each copy was printed on my home computer and the cover created and bound by hand. Each copy was different and specific to the person I was gifting, but I was realizing that what I really wanted was to surrender this collection to the world. This book has gone through many transitions, each representing an expansion of my own relationship with my writing and myself. And yet, at its foundation, it has written itself, my hands simply the road for the literal application.

I stand in a place in myself where writing is a sacred tool, a journey, and has the potential to create a road to manifest my heart's deepest desires. It can be used to open a dialogue and remember the relationship with

Self that is always available. It is the creative expression of Self in literal form. Standing in that place, I am never sure where the movement of the pen across the paper will take me and am often completely in awe that any of the resulting beauty came out of me. Yet, I can feel the words on the page create a movement in me that I can only describe as true.

As I now stand in a place where these words are being released to the world, I find I am humbled at everything that has had to move in my world, both outer and inner, to bring me to this moment. It is my prayer that, as you wander through the following pages, you will find some inspiration in what is presented.

FREEDOM

Falling through rivers of tears I find a light
glimmering, glowing, pulsing.
Remembering, I am
the light in my heart that loves me deeply.

Everywhere I look I am flying, wild, soaring.
Everywhere movement ensues
and I cannot drink it fast enough.

Doors open and are gone.
Love spills out and paints a new picture
....orange, red, yellow, green, blue, purple....
Vividly arranging themselves in the world,

Moving at the speed of my heart.

TRUTH

Dancing through chords of unconsciousness
I finally see truth.
like a light shining in the darkness
simple, bold and true.

Always there, just waiting for me to see it,
it ebbs and flows but is always there.
Alive. Remembering. Flowing. Loving.
Holding space.

And it amazes me.
It keeps me on the edge of my seat.
Holding me,
simply asking me to dance.

All that is required is for me to shift my eyes,
to turn my head slightly
and to see.

A breath, a moment.
Dancing softly to the rhythm of my soul.

FIRE

Fondling, dancing, loving, holding,
it is all one.
It is me.

I am connected,
I am a part,
I am life,
I am Creation.

Rounding my shoulders,
life leaps from me,
no thinking, no hearing,
no looking, just feeling,
just the ever loving of my soul.

Loving the truth, the essence of me,
I am Creation.

GRATITUDE

Giving myself in service,
walking the true path of my heart,
I stumble and fall
only to right myself in a breath.

I am learning. I am still a child.
There is so much to be aware of, so much to learn.
And I breathe
and find that still place at my center.

Tilting slightly to hear its voice
knowing it's there
listening, listening
it is so soft.

I find in the listening
a place hidden but not hiding.
I breathe, taking in all that I can
and release slowly.

I raise my arms to the sky
and under the sun and moon and stars
I pray out loud
"Thank You".

And these words do not seem like enough.
But in my heart they are.
They are from my heart,
ever opening to the new experience.

RESPECT

Rolling over the countryside
taking in the beauty of the landscape
I see the true essence of creation.
It is about finding beauty everywhere in everything.

I ride so close to the edge of my seat
I think I might fall off.

It is clear, it was here, paving the road before me.
Waiting patiently for my eyes to see it,
to feel it, to know it.

Everything connects.
Everything helps each other.
Everything moves together.

I must continue, as it does, stealthy and strong
across boundaries of the unknown,
taking nothing and everything along for the ride.

WORTH

Wandering through the woods
I search the sky for my friends.

Flying, soaring above me
over and through the clouds I find freedom.

I close my eyes and feel the movement
rising, moving all around.

I walk through a meadow
and by a stream and stop.

The meadow is quiet, still.
The stream is talking softly
as it glides over stones held by the earth.

It is beautiful.

COMMITMENT

Coming to age in the ways of the world,
Over all there is nothing.

Mounting tall the ways to freedom
I am flying higher and freer
and my Spirit sings.

To all it is unveiling,
the forward movement
of my soul.

Me. I am the one.
Above, Below, Within.
Ending nowhere I am free.

I hold my love close, not crushing or containing,
but gently moving towards freedom,
with all that I know to be true.

RESPONSIBILITY

Roundness of shoulders
and sharpness of ears
everything sees it all.

My heart pounds,
singing it's song loudly and fruitfully,
I listen.

Pounding gleefully,
I open further to the song.
Open wounds are gone.

Nodding....I follow.
I know this is my truth
I let go.

Singing, praying, opening, moving, evolving.
It is with love that I listen and love that I walk.
Bending slightly but always knowing
feeling my truth.

I cry.
Tears flow.
I let go and move with the wind.

Limber and strong,
flexibly grounded
in the Creators love,

I am one,
I am not alone.
I am one,
I am not separate pieces.

Yesterday is no more
There is only now
and I choose to follow.

FIRE OF CREATION

The fire of my dreams
gives birth, it seems.

Moving, moving, ebbing, flowing,
swirling, rushing, lapping, knowing.

Ripples open up to life that is creating life,
And I am standing in the center of it all.

Hands are held, bodies shaken,
lips touch and eyes awaken.

Breath stirs, shifts happen,
Remembering truths, speaking passion.

HEART

Helping me see, helping me breathe
I am grateful for it all.

Everything wanders & moves.
I breathe...
          and breathe again.

A voice heard. A feeling felt. A movement begun.
Rising up, turning, spinning, dancing....I am one.

Tired my legs are
but the inside knows there are
no limits, no boundaries, no end.
Only the truth and moving on.

INTEGRITY

In the days that come
I wander aimlessly.
Not knowing where or who I am
or when I'm going.

Never before
have I approached such a path
with remarkable willingness
and love.

I dream of touching my truth,
of knowing it intimately
and bringing that to every moment
of my every day human life.

A mystery made mastery.
A gift held soft and grateful -
eternally grateful.

Knowing what is waiting
I ease myself up and around.
It is the center of a round universe.
Creation waking up.

Moving together toward a goal.
Over, over, over.
I look, wondering what I will see.
And it is all right there in front of me.

Working over tender giving mutual love of all.
Amazed at what I find
I know there is more
and I yearn for it all.

DISCIPLINE

Directions taken
and movement made.
I wonder what it's all about.

Tender movement
coming to fruition.
Following through all the time.

In between, in places unknown,
piled high with doubt,
Layers of love unbind the ties.

Into darkness with a light.
Nocturnal living is a choice
and emptiness abates.

HONOR

Helping me find my way
I realize I am not alone.

What is around the next corner?
It is unknown,
but only unknown until it is known.

It is truth, it is honesty,
it is love, it is gratitude,
it is bigger than never before seen.

It is that love of all things, all of Creation,
that which I can hope only to know someday
but which I already know.

It is round and luminous and pulsating,
rolling over and over.
It is everything.

It is loving me and loving all things,
all life all truth, and knowing I am part of it all.
I am connected, I am part of the center.

DREAM

Divine intervention
rumbling in the clouds.

Everlasting,
    ever-loving,
        embracing.

Ample, able, amusing, alive
many times around.

Soundless, sound-full, synchronized...
Loved.

WARRIOR

Winding his way through the woods
he stumbles and finds a tree.
His horse stops. He stops.
It is a great Oak.

Acorns on the ground all around.
He kneels and prays.
His heart beats loudly and gladly.
This tree is a gift.

Round and beautiful,
the wind blows through the branches
moving the leaves
and speaking to his heart.

He is ready for the challenges,
he is ready to stand up
and claim his place.

He is ready to fight,
if necessary, to maintain it.
His heart sings.

He is grateful
for this beautiful gift
of his life
for it is truly a gift to behold.

He will battle
if necessary
but mostly he will love,
remembering his heart.

HUMILITY

Humbleness abounds all around,
dancing, spinning, twirling.

Across the room I see it.
Colors wrapped up like wisteria vines in a tree.

It is all so beautiful
My breath catches.
I wonder and call.

My heart flutters. My gratitude surfaces.
I kneel down with arms outstretched.

I breathe the earth. I sing my gratitude.
The wind takes me and I fly.
Soaring—my Spirit soaring.

I feel alive
like I've never been alive before
in my life.

My eyes are closed
but I can see just fine.

I know this is where it begins.
I know this is where I start.

This is where I learn to stand up.
This is where I learn to love myself
and all things in creation.

This is where I remember yesterday,
yearning for more.

FRIENDS

Frantically searching for what life really means,
racing through memories of misspent youth
and seemingly wasted time,
I find my vision becomes cloudy.

Evolution takes hold
and soon I start remembering
nothing is as dear to me
as the teachers along the way.

Then I am discovering
doors that were always there
but somehow disappearing just out of reach,
lost in the illusion.

Something holds me still,
and at last I can see
what was there all the time.

LOVE

Lingering in dreams,
my heart sings.
Above, below, within.

Over time and boundaries it speaks,
telling stories with truths.

Vulnerable, I am, to how it moves me,
and I hear a voice that melts me.

Everything changes
and what I find
when the spinning stops

is Love.

INTENT

I stand up.
I know my truth.
It is loud, clear and strong.

My heart screams notes to my mind
so soft it lifts me.

I walk
knowing every movement is truly
a choice from my heart.

It is all my heart's desire
for my evolution.

Entering everywhere
I carry this information with me.
It is my truth

and I cannot get near the edge
without feeling it ask me to be clear.

I know what the next terrific step is.
I know how to walk and where to put my feet
and it is freeing.

FAMILY

Fondly reaching into memories of days gone by
I stumble on the truth...and let go.

All there, waiting for me to see.
All there, just holding space.

Many holding hands out to the sky...to the earth.
I start to cry for it had been unknown,
like something at the edges of my consciousness,
disappearing when acknowledged.

Yet, when I stand here, in the center
and breathe into the unfolding,

Magic happens...
And I am surrounded by nothing but love.

DANCING TREES

Dancing trees
in the pale moonlight.

I take a breath
and my soul takes flight.

Twirling, spinning, softness all around,
to nothing am I bound.

Freedom sings a song of sweet release,
dissonant chords and finally....
Peace.

EAGLE'S VOICE

It is your own sacredness
that you are so afraid of.

It is your own strength and wisdom
that makes you run and hide.

See into the shadows of your soul with my eyes.
See the truth.

See and experience your own beauty.
Fly.

THRESHOLD

Wind softly whipping through my hair,
I close my eyes and am standing at the edge of me.
Looking out over the darkness,
looking for some sign of life.

There is something, but my eyes cannot find it.
I can feel it though,
pulsing through the thicket of my experience,
breathing a beat that makes me sing.

Eyes still closed I open my mouth,
not sure what to expect,
and hear a sound so beautiful
tears well up from the depths of my heart,
moving so strongly my breath catches in my throat;
yet it is all me, singing clearly.

It is the voice of love in my heart singing loudly.
And tears softly begin to trace trails
down my cheeks.

It is my Spirit searching for its freedom.

The drumming becomes louder, it is all I can hear.
I open my eyes and there is still darkness,
yet it is so full of possibility
I can touch truth everywhere.

It is the dreams for my life
moving, taking shape and breathing life into me.
I am dreamed, I am breathed and I am loved.

SUNSET

As sunset dawns and I turn to lay my weary head
in a place where the movement stops,
I am drawn into another place
where I can fly free and wild.

The fire in me burns and pulses,
lapping at everything I know, asking me to let go.

I close my eyes, take a breath
and with a powerful exhale
let the heat rise and move,
taking with it all that I've left behind.

I am no more that person who stood here wondering,
I am simply me, knowing.

HOME

Standing here,
standing everywhere
I begin to see
the ever-expanding glow of me.

It has taken a long time,
longer than
I would like to admit or
look in the direction of.

But, I have circled around
back to the opportunity
I had before,
back to now.

Looking in your eyes the struggle fades
and all that's left is the knowledge
that I am standing here
choosing a life that opens all my doors.

I am coming home.

BEAUTY UNFOLDING

Can I undo what has been done
    with a flick of my wrist,
    a blink of my eye,
    or simply laying a finger upside my nose?

Can I choose a different outcome
    by simply wanting it to be different
    and imagining who I would be?

Can I round up the truth of me
    and send it flying off into the stratosphere
    while just standing here taking it all in?

Can I ask for what I want
    and know absolutely that it is mine
    even before it gets here?

Reaching out a hand
    and gracefully cracking open
    the jar of disbelief,

My eyes do finally see
    that Beauty has taken root
    and flowered.

The growth of the beautiful
    opens wide
    the certain knowing of Love.

DEATH, MY FRIEND

There is this friend I know
that has a way of showing how he feels
with simple moves and warm embraces
and truth oozing from every pore.

He walks next to me with sparkling eyes,
looking for the perfect moment
to spread his loving arms and
transform my world into something new.

He always makes his presence known
but never in a way I've seen before.
He never comes when I'm sure he will,
mostly when I'm not ready, and sometimes
leaves me standing alone.

He likes the large and dramatic scenes
knowing he can crack everything open,
removing any sense of the familiar,
then agilely taking his leave for places unknown.

He has also walked through my life
gently purring and kissing a cheek,
breathing new life into places forgotten,
and illuminating that which I was sure was lost.

Unshakable in what moves him,
he gracefully does his one simple job:
transforming this thing I am
into all that I love.

He is my friend,
my ally if you will,
standing strongly at my side,
always at the ready and always knowing,
there is beauty in letting go.

THE WORLD ACCORDING TO ME

I will never be
interesting enough
to be a reality show contestant,
or desperate enough
to be on Jerry Springer.

I will never be
someone else's dream date,
or the girl who makes pies
and pastry and lies
for all of her perfect dinner guests.

And I will never be
adored
for all my radiant beauty
or adorned
with rings of flowers
celebrating my oozing femininity.

I will never be
the greatest
singer, poet, lover or friend
or the most desired philanthropist
for my ability to transcend.

I will never be seen
as the perfect being
visible only in my mind's eye,
yet, hopelessly
falling short every time.

And I will never be
what I secretly fear I am,
damaged, alone and invisible,
and the biggest fraud
around.

What I will be, however
is what I gratefully am,
Me, I said,
no more and no less
than all of that
in this very moment.

For Further Reading

Here are a few books and individual poems that have assisted in my personal development both as a human and writer and continue the theme begun in this book. Enjoy.

Books:

The Exquisite Risk, Mark Nepo
The Dance, Oriah Mountain Dreamer
The Way of the Peaceful Warrior, Dan Millman
The Camino, Shirley MacLaine

Poems:

Variation on a Theme by Rilke, Denise Levertov
Care Take this Moment, Epictetus
Love After Love, Derek Walcott
Unlived Life, Dawna Markova
Guest House, Rumi

Heartfelt Gratitude

There are many to thank who have assisted me on my journey and, whether they know it or not, have contributed in some way to the outcome of this book. These last few pages are just a moment in time to express the depth of the joy those relationships have provided. Following are just a few of those acknowledgments, the ones that can actually be put into words.

...to my mother and older sisters for always teaching me how to be clear about what my choices are and what I want. I am grateful for the continuing lessons.

...to Little Night Bear for providing a place to start over, again.

...to Stone Shield for the assistance with the literal process of putting this book together. It has been quite a journey and I'm grateful for your support and quiet encouragement.

...to Rainbow Owl for sharing your amazing editing skills and for teaching me how to find that gentle place within and the power of meeting myself and the world standing in that place.

...to Standing Bear for always being a place to explore an amazing array of boundless ideas and being an immeasurable source of support, even when the ideas are uninspired.

...to Medicine Pipe for consistently and lovingly asking me the hard questions that necessarily require diving in and going deeper. What a gift.

...to Standing Wolf for the perpetual reminder that just because things die does not mean they end. Nor does it mean they will end up as they have in my past.

...to Talking Wolf for standing in front of me and showing me how great strength can be found when you are willing to unabashedly fall down face first, especially when you're uncertain if you will ever be able to get back up again.

...to Dancing Fire for helping me find the way to laugh at myself and reminding me that it is an incredibly necessary and powerful tool to continue moving forward.

...to Drumming Wolf for helping me solve every problem in the world in an hour on the phone and for always not giving a rodent's behind what my ego has to say about anything, ever.

...to my Raven Sisters for the tears, the laughter and the process for which my appreciation continues to grow moment by moment. Thank you for taking this journey with me.

...to the rest of my Spiritual Family, my sisters and brothers who continually support me in so many unspoken ways on every step of my journey, I am loving all of you.

...to Looking Hawk for standing with me even when I refuse to see I have feet, for teaching me that "relationship" is not a 4-letter word, for gently reminding me that I have always known how to leap fearlessly, and for the unending journey of guidance, support and Love . You are an inspiration, a beautiful reflection of what is possible and a precious gift for which I am humbly grateful. Thank you for seeing Me.

Many thanks to all who continue to stretch me, guide me and Love me in every way possible. I am deeply grateful.

About the Author

StarShield has been a student of Native American Shamanic and Toltec traditions for over eight years. She brings a perspective of heart and truth to her work, creating the space for the manifestation of her heart's deepest desires. Her writing practice has become the road for these desires to travel. Expanding through her personal writing practice, StarShield created Writing Medicine as a way to share her journey and promote the utilization of writing as a spiritual tool. Writing Medicine includes writing workshops, a monthly writer's group, individual coaching and more, all designed as a way to open a dialogue and remember the relationship with Self that is always available.

StarShield currently resides in Nashville where she writes, facilitates workshops, organizes speaking engagements, and performs her poetry at an occasional open mike night.

For more information about StarShield, Writing Medicine, or to order additional copies of this book, please contact StarShield at www.writingmedicine.com.